'Let me make you something to eat'
Author Nabeela Saghir
This edition published in 2022 by Fawn Press.
Cover design & illustration by Megan Laura Roberts
ISBN 978-1-3999-2268-5
All rights reserved. No part of this publication may be reproduced, by any means without prior permission of the copyright owner.
Printed and bound by Kingate Press, Birmingham, UK.

*"Poetry that takes you by the hand
and leads you into the woods"*

FAWN PRESS

Contents

Praise for 'Let me make you something to eat' … 4

Dupatta	6
Thoughts on a plane between countries	7
Back when the sun was allowed to touch me	9
Black dots	10
Apricots	11
A dress for the living	12
In praise of silence	13
Plucked	14
A fantasy	15
All I know now	16
I saw you in the National Museum of Warsaw long after you passed	17
Little parcels	18
Urdu lesson	19
Tongues in slow motion	20
Battleground	21
Ode to the mirror carp	22
She / you / i	25
Marigold baby	26
The sea is the sky's reflection	27
Working bees back to the hive	28

Acknowledgements … 28
About the author … 30

Praise for 'Let me make you something to eat'.

"Nabeela Saghir's poetry is filled with rich fragrance and deep colour. Intricate threads of language and memory intertwine here, in a delicate study of daughterhood and longing."

-Nina Mingya Powles

"Let me make you something to eat is poetry as an invitation, as evocation and as a heartfelt act of making of space around the table to be nourished and made whole in food, memory, and family. In Saghir's precise, enriching and lyrical poems, language itself is a feast – the tongue and body found hungry for words and the rich physicality that connects to daily rituals, through daughterhood and motherhood, and to the precious stories we all carry within us. These absorbing and tender poems skilfully appeal to our senses and our hearts – Nabeela Saghir is a truly gifted writer we should all be watching out for in future."

-Jane Commane

"Nabeela Saghir carefully crafts together language, culture and womanhood. Each word has been painstakingly chosen and woven. Saghir's poetry makes you travel from Karachi, through Classrooms, Museums and Kitchens to discovering one's own essence with precise and lyrical poems. Nabeela Saghir traces intergenerational conversations, healing and femininity holding great beauty but also power in her words. 'Let me make you something to eat', will make a fantastic read for those who want to see an intersection of language and bilingual poetry."

-Rupinder Kaur

"In this intricate collection, English and Urdu flirt together around the universal love language of food. Its undercurrents of darkness make the intimate taste of every poem all the more needed, and all the more nourishing. Saghir's delicate imagery gives every fruit, every vegetable, every morsel a soul, and a story - indeed, she makes food a living thing, and a loving thing. I am full, after reading."

-Jasmine Gardosi

Dupatta

It swats mosquitos on the taxi ride through Karachi.
It's a basket for gold pears and books, a blanket for the monsoon.
It's a fluttering around your face, a shelter from dirt and heat
and eyes
like a moth clutching light it wraps its weight around you
its threads tangled in hair, a knot I pull tight.
It's what cradles us, carries me down to the kitchen in its arms
and whispers,
let me make you something to eat.

Thoughts on a plane between countries

Sugarcane

You sat along cotton-lined fields,
guava trees by your side before we came
to crack your spine.
My uncle cradled you in, the echo
of an off-white weeping.
I remember teeth, how we tore skin
clean off your body, the sacrilege leaving an ache
in my jaw.

                    You were a cane still felt,
                            like splintered feathers,
                    half-dressed.

                                              Ganna

                            I ask mother to repeat:
                                    Ganna.
                                    Gha / nna.

                  You sit in my throat like a paperweight,
                                  a heavy *h*.
                              You burn, so I stop.

Gha / nna.
Say it with jazbah, build each sound
before curling the tongue

and hold –
like a stone lodged, not yet ready
to soften.

Back when the sun was allowed to touch me

My body summoned by the water's belly,
dress ballooning around my legs, those skinny girlish legs –
I was halfway to the pond's bottom before my Nani
pulled me out, smoothed down my dress, and handed me an orange
sliced in the shape of my mouth.

I brought it to my teeth, juice sliding down knees
before I grabbed a fistful of fabric, hitched it high, and let the heat
soak up the sticky glaze.

Black dots

She drags her hair to the back of her skull,
guides her fingers through its dark cherry knots
through the sound of a plate crashing, and a dying lilac
somewhere close by.

She stretches it flat and slick
wondering in which light she could let a strand unfurl.

A chair scratches against tiles downstairs
as she pulls her last curl straight, pins it tight
to her scalp but when reaching the kitchen she finds
the crockery already thrown out –

and her mother's head, swaying, a plucked poppy,
hair combed into a small neat gift.

Apricots

A fruit in the shape of a birthmark,
khubani – the word would roll off my mother's tongue
and fall into my lap.

She'd help me pull my sleeves up,
thin wrists, clean hands.
I remember when she let me hold a knife for the first time
and how the small sunrise in my hand
flashed in its reflection.

I sliced, hit the stone twice
before it bled onto the board. As a child I called it sun juice,
it glazed my elbows, gave a shine to my fingers –

khubani, it tickled my throat,
pushed its way down, hungry to settle. I blushed a few years later
when I asked again: is it *khubani* or *qhurbani*?
I can't remember. And after a moment my mother said,
    I guess it's both.

*Khubani: apricot in Urdu
*Qhurbani: sacrifice in Urdu

A dress for the living

Grief is spinning in a dress stitched by your mother's mother
years after the funeral.
For your wedding she had said.
It's hard to imagine it now, her weaving through markets
searching for headpins,
a seam unpicker, tape, metallic thread
pearls, mesh, beading for the hem –
the movement like a chant, a wave swaying, a chest rising.
The same way her hands cut, fold, twist, bleed
I'll pleat a sonnet into an origami bird
to fly towards your breath –
the wind will catch you when you lean into flight.
What fabric did they bury her in?
I hope it was joy.

In praise of silence

Stench of the lily opens in full. You place lemon zest, two drops of thyme and almond oil into a glass, a slight chip in its side. Your fingertips are cold. I don't flinch. Sitting on the edge of your bed I almost slink to the carpet.

You avoid the lids and the neck. Too soft? You never tell. I ask why two drops, you sigh into my face. There's a strangeness in the smearing, the turning, repeating, until a nail catches my lip. I don't flinch. My left eye swells, hairs flutter in the heat of your bedroom lamp. I can't see where the sadness has settled in the air but don't you feel it smirk, feel it eat your elbows and wrists till you are nothing but open-ended artery

                and hands,
                            against your baby's face.

Are you okay, mother? There's blood on the carpet. Let me bandage your finger, glass can be cruel when unwatched. Pass me a wet cloth, I'll fall to the carpet and scrub, bleach it back to lily-white, just as you like.

Plucked

I plucked its body, the oval-eyed dark bruised thing
and bit – scrunched my nose at the taste

wondered if your first time was the same, the way
its dull skin collected rain and summer dust.

Did you feel it too? Rolling in my palm, heavy
with black blood. I let it fall, down into the throat of a lilac

so white, so bare, bright teeth –
I crushed my damson with the heel of my hand

let my veins stain purple. *Make it soft,* you said,
like mother's favourite jam.

A fantasy

We call it bhindi, I think
or okra, in English.

I always knew when the vegetable had found its way into the pot.
Its smell crawls through the kitchen – slow, and heavy, and thick.

Bhindi.

The word a rock under bare feet. Scaly as though at any moment
it's going to rise and bite.

I start tugging at the mint my mother has tasked me on.
The act of lifting, and pulling, and placing

it into a bowl is concentrated,
safe.

I look to my mother and wiggle my nose as she pulls
her shawl closer, and laughs.

All I know now

Did you know it takes five weeks to hear a baby's heartbeat
in the right womb, and three to ten years for a tree to bear fruit?

A body is a greenhouse, after all.
It has air circulation, well-drained soil, space for a whole sun.

Warmth is a weight felt most in the belly.
It bursts and says *here, I kept this heat for you.*

                                      Now, here? This is what I know:
                            it's spring. I'm starved. A pear hangs by a thread

                                          you've let go of my hand
                                     and my heart still beats, warm.

I saw you in the National Museum of Warsaw long after you passed

but you are no Orange Vendor.[1] You'll find no citrus under those nails, and why are you draped in autumn when you hold heat so well?[2] Those are not your hands Nani, how did you get inside a frame so small? The doors are closing now but don't fret, you are no babciu, no mother of my mother but a sun tucked away[3], stitched into the seams of my back pocket.

---

[1] 'Jewish Woman with Oranges' by Aleksander Gierymski (1881)
[2] Who are you?
[3] Which version will I remember?

Little parcels

A slow gold burn, lamb-and-pea-filled shells
all day I imagine their flakes falling from lip to plate
spiced, smooth, a prayer the size of my mother's palm.
Their journey begins at 8am in strange kitchen light,
the sky's hangover from Sehri stretches
through the window, onto the floured worktop.
Little white stars stirred with oil and salt.
My mother peels the dough off her fingers
washed in time for Zuhr, a midday kneeling before
it starts again set to medium heat, a marigold
blooming from the hob infused with cumin
and fennel, ginger, crushed coriander, chilli to taste.
She lines the dough with meat and builds,
a careful crossing and folding before it slides
into crisp heat – it's Maghrib now.
I place the aam, sliced in the shape of crescents
on the dining room table, sticky date syrup and lassi
in place for when my mother carries them in.
Sizzling slick with light grease spotted with black pepper
and then we wait, and wait, for the first bite of samosa
to stitch itself to tongue, to shed its pastry skin
spread its curled wing, newly born, just in time for Iftar.

Urdu lesson

You don't have to smile. The corners of your mouth
would unravel, reveal a white too sharp for these walls.

Start at the corner of the room shaped like a fist and
work your way through the halls. Avoid the stairs,

they're for the cracked pens and pages where ink blotted
a little too bright.

Did you pick up the cards? They were handed out
at the front desk. Some have pictures which I know

you won't like but you'd cling to the words I'm sure.
You're a glass-half-full-with-air type, your letters need space

for their equal echoing. Sometimes a mouth isn't
wide enough to hold all those chilke. Not chilka, chilke.

Good. You're learning. There is more than one husk inside
your body. You are made of a million tiny shells and

they all sit on your tongue. Don't do it just yet, wait.
Open when you're ready to smile all that white.

Tongues in slow motion

Alif l, or
sunrises,
gold-licked scar, or sword,
a tongue-to-teeth whisper in a baby's ear,
or wombs,
a weeping inside the walls of a

Masjid, or
a house holding air,
carpet carrying the weight of bones:
ammi or abbu's,
or five ways to hold my hand in the dark
instead of a

Maqas, or
legs crossing in sync,
qainchi in ammi's voice, scarlet on my lip,
or silver flames
caught in cupped palms, in prayer
before the final

Waqf-e-Taam, or
a perfect stop in breath, in sunsets,
the mouth of a moulvi,
or a quiet leaf,
the one sitting in my blood,
asleep, perhaps. ◯

Battleground

How should I play? Do I hide, or hunt?
Do what you always do when you're in trouble.

I look up, find your face in the stands.

What would you do?
Eat, of course.

I reach into my pocket, start clicking the shells off pistachios –
their green tongues scatter, a hushed scream, a standing ovation.

I bow.

Ode to the mirror carp

I.
Look! How they spin, fins vibrating and O-mouthed,
scales beating in a blood-rush.

Mother asks: have you ever heard a fish scream?
It's like a body rupturing, eating itself whole before re-entering the womb.

This is how girl becomes woman.

II.
There's a burning in their stomachs only death can cure.
Their hunger? Watch it rage, it's the only thing that draws fish out of water.

See their bodies pirouette for the last time,
they'll stop squirming soon.

This is how a woman lives.

.

III.
Mother reels them in.
I have her hands – I know, mine are just as impossible to hold.

Dinner will be served soon.
I open and close my mouth, and swim, and swim.

This is how we survive.

She / you / i

That feeling, hold it, it's a warmth only you feel. Let the half cut lemons roll and spill onto your dress, your lace and pearl neckline, off-white, their yellow ink in your hands –don't limp your wrist, lift it higher to that pink mouth and stay like that, eyes like a moon cut in two, and even when I grow and wilt, remember me like this, in our room, surrounded by tiny suns.

Marigold baby

The rioting marigolds
are deep in the pit of my stomach, each petal carries
spots of blood, each a swollen flame;

does a womb of amber
burn as much as a needle through an eye,

                                        in a building made of flesh, how much ash
                                                                  can I be?

I hope the blood clings to the needle,
that you walk the folded lines of my city map, that all the orange
scars the sky black;

I hope the glowing marigolds and liquid eyes will be ours.
I'll blow chaos into each open mouth, feel pollen powdering skin,

                                                 let me show you how much ash
                                                                 I can be.

The sea is the sky's reflection

'Nothing except a single green light, minute and far away'
- The Great Gatsby by F. Scott Fitzgerald

A girl is born with a tilt,
an imbalance inside her bones.
She watches the world come full circle each year:
how trees drop their dead parts, how they return to root in Spring.

A girl searches for mirrors
to angle straight.
A traffic light, a neighbour in a sage dress, moss climbing brick,
a sign
coffee cup logos, greenflies, neon signs.

The green will grow back in the shape of a glittering minaret
minute and far away,
close enough to almost touch.

Working bees back to the hive

Lyric taken from 'When the Family Flies In' by Julia Jacklin

Prise the tremor from underneath my ribs.
It'll beat for a moment
and then it won't.
You'll carry it with you like a dead baby
or a memory you can't unsee.
Find a chisel in the shape of a mother
and start with the left ventricle.
It doesn't have to be perfect, just new.
Dig for the skin that shrunk
pull at flesh and vein, mould till it feels like yours.
Keep it close, carry it to full-term.
Your chest will know when it's time,
it'll call, an invitation, a need not a want.
Precision is key. Use the tweezers I left
in the bottom drawer.
Light will pour in once you're open.
Lower it now, quick but gentle like a quiet gaze
and tuck behind its new cage.
A body has to enter its own grave
before it can breathe again.
You won't have to wait long before my heart is yours entirely.
First we'll shiver, then beat
and beat.
We'll be family again, loveable even.

Acknowledgements

I would like to thank Jane Commane for believing in my poems right from the beginning of my writing journey. Being accepted onto the Dynamo Mentoring Scheme not only elevated my work but boosted my confidence. It was during this time that I finally felt like I deserved to call myself a real poet.

A special thank you to Nina Mingya Powles for taking the time to run a shadowing session with me. It was Nina's thoughtful and constructive feedback given in her 'Language Diaries' online course that pushed me to incorporate Urdu into my poems. Lastly, I am forever grateful to Nina for publishing 'Little Parcels' in Bitter Melon Press as part of the Stay Home Diary project in 2020.

'The sea is the sky's reflection' takes a quote from The Great Gatsby by F. Scott Fitzgerald (Charles Scribner's Sons, 1925). 'I saw you in the National Museum of Warsaw long after you passed' takes inspiration from the painting 'Jewish Woman with Oranges' by Aleksander Gierymski (1881), and 'Working bees back to the hive' takes a lyric from 'When The Family Flies In' by Julia Jacklin (2019).

The warmest thank you to my high school English teacher Miss Mathews who had every faith that I will be published one day. I couldn't have done it without her endless support. To Jack, for listening to my ideas and saying all the right things when I needed them the most, and to Megan Laura Roberts for the gorgeous artwork.

To my wonderful Editor and friend Scarlett Ward Bennett. Her passion and work ethic is the driving force behind a truly magical press – I'm so happy my poems found a home here. Finally, thank you to my family for being my biggest cheerleaders, especially my mum who always has time to make me something to eat.

About the author.

Writing on food, family and belonging, Nabeela Saghir is a poet and copywriter raised in the West Midlands and currently based in North-West London.

Nabeela was selected for the Dynamo Mentoring Scheme run by Nine Arches Press in 2020, and has work featured in The Hellebore Press and Bitter Melon Poetry.